Let Widows Be Widows

poems

Laura LeHew

Attention schools and businesses: for discounted copies on large orders, please contact the publisher directly.

For information contact:

Unsolicited Press

Portland, Oregon

www.unsolicitedpress.com

orders@unsolicitedpress.com

619-354-8005

Cover Design: Kathryn Gerhardt

Editor: S.R. Stewart

ISBN: 978-1-956692-06-8

This book is dedicated to "mom" Janet Putnam Morrison.

TABLE OF CONTENTS

1

Trinity	13
The Old Ones	15
Are You The Sister?	17
Driving Through Wetlands	19
Scars	20
3 Days Prior To April Fools' Through Friday The 13th—A Fortnight Of Reckoning In The Year Of The Dragon	22
Heritability	23
Olly Olly Oxen Free	24
Possessing No Physiological Function	26
Marrow	27
Eventually, There Is Silence	29
We Have Time Though	30
A Face Held In Darkness	31
Be Aware, Be Prepared	32
Some Assembly May Be Required	34

Let Widows Be Widows   36

2

Imagine   40

Except By Chance   42

The Sad Man   43

Closure   45

Emphysema   47

An Invisible Fluvial Zoo   48

Three Funerals And A Wedding   49

Going Under   55

June Bug   57

Losing Monday—   60

Tornado Alley   62

Decomposing Dad   64

Prelude   65

Points Of Attraction   67

Wraith   69

A Distance To Be Traveled   70

En Route   72

Holding Up   74

I Love Teamwork, As Long As I'm In Charge 76

Persimmon 78

3

Riding Backwards On Trains 84

Elegy For Twenty-One Million Women 85

11×10^6 86

Meanwhile 88

Recounting The Dead 90

The Porcelain Bowl 94

A Stranger Asks For Help With The Lettuce 95

/ & | 97

The Fate For Which We Must Prepare 98

Ctrl-Alt-Del 100

What We Give Up 101

Salt 103

Self Portrait As Our Nation's Capitol 105

4

The Moon Is A Harsh Mistress 108

For A Moment 109

Raven Song Crow Song   110

A Stone   111

Topaz, The Grumpinator   112

Police—Do Not Cross   114

In View Of The Fact That; Considering;

    Inasmuch As   115

After The Rapture   117

Insatiable   119

Light Like A Star   121

Flame Point   123

No More Sky Diving   124

When The Trine Between The Moon And Mercury

    Tempers The Vibe   126

October Rains   127

5

Ghost Ranch   130

In My Sky Of Sand   131

Ida By Moonlight   133

Elegy On The Death Of A Friend   134

After The Eulogy   137

Catching Up   138

A Grim Reaper   139

"Cousin" Larry   140

What The Dead See   142

The Bird Of Time   143

November   144

On The Edge Of Dusk   146

Approximation   148

Proportional Relationships   149

Untitled   150

Cumulonimbus   151

1

hospice
a flight attendant announces
the door is closing

TRINITY

because words were left unsaid
& other words inked & inked & always
deleted

because dissipating rain etches
black ice & other treacherous
circumstances

the husband working late into the night
the wife on the couch, shopping
QVC

body without purpose
the husband contemplating dissolution,
a lover, settles into drink

body without dreams
the wife defiant trying & trying not
to surrender

among the alder, wild trillium
overrun the path, overtake the
hillside

nobody should have to
bury a child

THE OLD ONES

women like so many
snowflakes
ice crystals
falling &

falling
collide with earth
transcendent
skin opens

china-white femurs
hips, vertebrae fracture
the snow of women
drifts deep & wide

carpets their husbands—lovers
long gone to ground—
old ones, arms legs splay
etch angels into frost

I mistake the stairs for
floor   wonder if this is
how it began for my
grandmother

a yellow crocus blooms just
outside my window

ARE YOU THE SISTER?

the nurse asks. 23 hours after another
test, an ultrasound, 3 months after
the MRI, after 17 blood work-ups,
after her doctor retires & my sister,
Karen, is in limbo.

      Yes, I say, *I am the sister, the guardian,*
yes I say *I have questions* but the nurse
isn't listening, the nurse is already referring
me to a surgeon. A specialist.
      The mass—whom I call Frederick—

Frederick, it seems, has substantially enlarged.
He is a blind man, devoid of his white tipped cane,
on an accelerating bus careening out of control. He
becomes invasive, continues without stopping—
unbound.

                    30 minutes later
the surgeon's office calls & a new nurse
gives me the 1st available appointment 2 weeks in
the future, 1 day before I head home for my 40th
high school reunion.

Don't worry she says—*everything is already preapproved bring your questions then.* She says without giving me the opportunity to say but I have questions—a million questions. *Bring your sister, she shouldn't do this alone.*

DRIVING THROUGH WETLANDS

two sisters
glide down the highway
will it hurt?   *not today*

sisters offkeyloud
merge Petula Clark pastpresent
forget all your troubles   *forget all your cares*

two great white egrets
ease into riversky
meld   into shadowsun

SCARS

underneath your beard
throat chakra to heart chakra
vertical like an earthworm
bruises already feathering yellow

I see you in a blue
hospital gown
monitors and wires
transpose your tats

I hadn't recalled
hadn't ever given voice
my nephew 6 months old
turning blue

this same opening up
of his tender heart
pinking, his life—
a resurrection

Joe crying in a crib
John at the VA taking selfies
Amazon Photos sends me a reminder
on this day 14 years ago—

a long-necked Bud Light
in a parking lot, one niece
getting her nails done, one
niece getting her hair done

my father's funeral

3 DAYS PRIOR TO APRIL FOOLS' THROUGH FRIDAY THE 13th—A FORTNIGHT OF RECKONING IN THE YEAR OF THE DRAGON

I want not to have reinjured my rotator cuff brooming
  record-breaking snow off trees the first days of spring
I want my fingers not to be numb
I do not want to sleep coffined in pillows the shroud of blankets
  angry against my skin
After my sister's 2nd mammogram I want the technician not to
  say we're doing an ultrasound
I want the nurse not to come in and say the doctor will see you
  now
I want the doctor not to say … biopsy …
I don't want to explain to my sister that she might have cancer
I want my sister not to say *ok that sounds fine*
I want the scheduling nurse not to say 2 weeks should probably
  be ok
I want her primary doctor not to have called that very day not to
  have checked to see if we were happy with the progress
I want no more bad news
no more friends with heart attacks, strokes, bad divorces, dead
  dogs
prostate cancer, mothers hospitalized with pneumonia
no more posthumous emails no
I want my phone to stop ringing
I want it all to be lies

HERITABILITY

for my brother Don LeHew 1947 - 2010

I met you when I was 40
I met you because I was the black sheep of the new family
I met you because you were the black sheep of the old family
I met you at a Denny's
I met you without knowing what you looked like
and when you walked in I *knew* you were my brother
I met you and you were wearing the same red Hawaiian shirt
  dad had
I met you and you told the same joke dad told before I left
I met you and you asked me why dad loved me and not you
I met you and you asked me what you had done that was so bad
I met you with silence—a night moth lodged obsidian in my
  tongue
Later I sent you poems about a father who never loved his
  daughters
I sent you poems about a father who never loved his wives
I sent you poems about addictions, unknowing aunts, bruises
I sent you poems about love and the death of my cat Topaz
and your cat Topaz had just died
and you picked up the phone and called
and you told me to never live with regret
and you promised you'd come for a visit
but then a stranger called to tell me you would not

OLLY OLLY OXEN FREE

1.

I google you and find you dead or a health hazard
or a former athlete or LinkedIn or Facebooked (but I'm not)
also possibly wearing tight tan slacks
(which only you could pull off)

I google you and find out that you never
won a Senior National title in Olympic lifting
that there are similar people in places like Humble,
Kouts, Cheshire and Groom

I find pictures, your dead wife
but I never find you

2.

your peeps
confess you are
ablaze

I telephone you
get your 411

3.

you grab my hand
pull me near
whisper

I'm your knight
your white horse
I will always be there

4.

olly olly

POSSESSING NO PHYSIOLOGICAL FUNCTION

Some people name their cars—I
have named my uncontrollable rapidly growing cellular
 proliferation
the unforeseen unplanned unabortable
mid-life crisis unbaby
incubating in my kidney
Claudia

Is she one of those malignant little Goths
an offshoot of post-punk a vampire freak
or a mouthless pink Hello Kitty girl

Nobody expects stones to turn up growths

MARROW

after Denise Newman

pith of spine and cord marrow galvanizes inward
ligatures like filaments woven wet chain-link across the
  starless sky
unrest has no ideal or hematological order   think of cancer
and panic

a wolf spider on the end of neurons in tangerine twilight
like a stab in the brain that throbs with the words
3 months to live or *keeping a positive attitude*
        can blood itself be insufficient

poison oak   three leaves that
sear the flesh   step nimbly over   you feel
you are safe   you are fine, you are divergent   make a home
on the brow and do not look down

probe platelets each-every covetous dawn
primp just right just so—
in the evening probe again
another way to vary

he thinks living is wack
but often sighs
there's tedium in blood
and eternity

EVENTUALLY, THERE IS SILENCE

Baby lies coiled in the crook of my arm
nuzzling my face, each breath a bit uncertain
her paw on my face, she slows into sleep.

My mother crashed into the porcelain floor—a sleep
she would eventually never wake from. We sisters took up arms—
battling brain aneurism, lung cancer. We were young and
assuredly uncertain.

We did all that could be done, undone—everything uncertain
fired doctors, painted toenails, lied. And still she died in a
  fitful sleep;
we told her she would get well—staring at tubes, IVs, her
  purpling arms.

My arm snuggles you in tight listening for each inhalation,
exhalation, uncertain of sleep.

WE HAVE TIME THOUGH

this hand still misses
the glove of your fingers
misses the crook of your elbow
    couched in proximity
this thigh, twisty ankle, splay
of painted pink toenails
misses your counterparts
    misses wide screen, surround sound
finding a common ground
in a search for an elegant yet efficient Beretta
    misses your tongue its cascade
vowels, consonants, caramelized words
whispers held tightly—blown into ears
tongues, teeth—poetry nibbled
into the fold of the neck
    misses the swap of hats
stories written daily on Post-its
misses most egregiously
our ritual of coffee and
caress

A FACE HELD IN DARKNESS

after "Migrant Mother," (pea-picking camp), Dorothea Lange 1936

her children burrow into her
thinning frame into her
turned down smile
her left hand on her cheek
as if to hold in the questions
forehead etched with uncertainty

BE AWARE, BE PREPARED

We wind our way to Oroville,
to Plumas National Forest, my Integra racing
patches of sunlight and shadow.

We arrive early, hike Feather Falls
the lower loop is long and hard, we
do that first.

The cartilage in my left knee frays
and frays and as we crest
the second mile of the uphill grade—

anticipating ticks, poison oak, bears but not
a knee swollen solid, refusing
to bend.

The falls plunge
into a canyon, we swim
in snow melt.

My old cat has died. My elder friend
has died. A gathering, a clowder, a pride
of deaths.

Death the fine filament of a web
the startle etching my face, conjures
spider and bite and beauty and grace

and broken home. The Missouri River
raged brown and overwrought. My mother
charged us to *do something good*, sandbag

the *damnable* river. Staunch its flow. My mother
now long dead drove us to the edge.

SOME ASSEMBLY MAY BE REQUIRED

you are in denial
your eyes are hyacinth red
you page through your daughter's wedding album
you flood 1,000 lakes with tears
you lie
& you say it's about her
divorce
you buy a kayak
you buy an oar but
not a lifejacket not a helmet
ask *who wants to look through this with me*
one more time you fear
you might have missed something
you could have missed anything
you lost your house after your heart
attack
but now
submerged you ask & you ask & you ask
why not you
& already there is so much water
in the binder the hospital gave you to navigate around
your husband &
you get a purple *caregiver* ribbon—pin it on your long sleeve
you are so cold—your

friends all come to visit you crash into end-stage
you become proficient at chemo-day valet parking
at first you thought you would be the one to go
you confess your grief
you dry your eyes
hop up to make lasagna
his favorite
your husband suddenly has been diagnosed—
esophageal cancer, and you—
you wish you could remember if
you could swim

LET WIDOWS BE WIDOWS

●

speak not of her wintering
not of veins laced with snow
crescendoed tears
avalanche after
avalanche

●

silence
your squeam
regarding the tasks you're dealt
when you said you would
help

●

      blackberries—

●

even
while he was alive she

was widowed
his calling penultimate
loneliness her
gospel

●

generals, commanders
buried her wrenched
heart beside his

●

in still water
a lone blue heron forages
happenstance

2

IMAGINE

the phone ringing
the call to come home
juxtapose the relief of her release
nothing more to be done

imagine using frequent flyer miles for a free flight home
using Marriott points for a free hotel
negotiating the cost of a rental car for a week
the lines, the flights, tight connections, midnight arrivals

imagine your nephew in a black suit, crisp white shirt,
  yellow striped tie
a thunderstorm of tears as he weeps for his aunt who has just
  departed and
for those who have gone on before—Grandma Marcy, Paul's
  father,
Meagan's mother, Grandpa Don, your nephew's hand in
  yours throughout the Mass

imagine driving your rental to Jefferson Barracks
your procession waiting behind three other processions

to bury the Veterans
your nephew's hand on your arm

your grandson
holding a paper airplane
asking you *who shotted Aunt June*
imagine explaining a natural death

EXCEPT BY CHANCE

JULY

her boring hernia surgery ^ **1 6**—
she became extremely—excessively—very very ill **1 7**—
fever—agony—&—multi organ failure **1 8**—**1 9**
  2 0—**2 1**—**2 2**—**2 3**—**2 4**—
emergency surgery **2 5**—
wound reopened | left **2 5**—**2 6**—**2 7**—**2 8**—
open to disinfect—decontaminate & to watch | **2 5**—
  2 6—**2 7**—**2 8**—
to watch-spy-keep-an-eye-out-on | for *MRSA* **2 5**—
  2 6—**2 7**—**2 8**—
watch | for decay **2 5**—**2 6**—**2 7**—**2 8**—
| putrescence **2 5**—**2 6**—**2 7**—**2 8**—
continuous dialysis **2 5**—**2 6**—**2 7**—**2 8**—
an alabastered coma induced induced induced induced
  2 8—
calculate her awakening in [86,400 – 129,600] seconds
  tick-tick-tick by—but—**2 8**—**2 9**—**3 0**
she—has not yet—**3 1**
& then a slight grasp of her hand in mine ⌄ **1**

AUGUST

THE SAD MAN

for months now we pass him by
Monday, Wednesday, and Friday
mornings

he wears blue jeans a
blue jacket with rust trim
sometimes a blue stocking cap

his gait is slow and methodical
he ambles past our laughter and gossip
blind to bikes, newts, curious dogs

silence wraps around him
a melancholy cloak of invisibility
only his eyes betray him—

illuminate his unending sorrow I
want to reach out, hug him
tell him it will be alright

but I—we don't we
give him wide berth
hope his gloom

is not contagious

CLOSURE

for EWK

*Things are sweeter when they're lost. ... and when I got it it turned
to dust in my hand.* ~F. Scott Fitzgerald

We lie we
tell her
it's just
temporary

We—for her
own good We
tell her she *will*
come home

metastasized
    means she has some
while longer, some
            time left

but

the last day
I head for
work I
turn

around haunted I drive non-stop
dread fingers clutch the wheel I
call them then, her men—I
tell them to come before

too late

&
mother's hand
gnarled & brittle gentled
in mine I whisper stories over & over

katydid song tempos
the forest
the final sigh
listen—

EMPHYSEMA

nothing changes—
$10 to bribe a nurse
(1) Lucky Strike

AN INVISIBLE FLUVIAL ZOO

After the phone call luring me home, after I buried Janice's husband, after I visited Marie, lately resurrected from three weeks in a drug-induced coma, after the cold, after dealing with little sister's dementia, Dad's Alzheimer's, after the flu, after I was my nephew's daily respite caregiver, after Special Olympics, being pulled over and narrowly escaping a speeding ticket (which I'm sure I deserved), after Vicki's double mastectomy, Mark's father-in-law's cancer exploding out of the liver and into nodes and bones, after I got a late check-out, had lunch, navigated the rental's return, and somehow got to the airport early, after all that, I came to be a pebble lodged within the aquifer—I did not standby in hope of an earlier flight, didn't sail through the airport dodging kiosks, loose children, baggage.

THREE FUNERALS AND A WEDDING

1.

Rita's first husband
Jimmy Joe—Jimmy Lee—X Jimmy
is "hanging around" with Rita's
born again friend Gaye
so when Rita's father dies
Jimmy whoever shows up
at the funeral parlor
decked out in his best jeans
and cowboy boots sporting
a handlebar mustache and long
straggly beard
looks her up and
down leans in
for an un-forthcoming hug
hollers—*you look **GOOD***
for your age—
you don't look at all like your momma—hell
you didn't even get fat
stays for the entire viewing
hits on all the single women

despite daggers blasting from Rita's
second husband Dave's eyes
and overtly loud rude
comments from the family

2.

the umbilical cord gets kinked
Margaret's friend Katie is having a C-section
Katie's husband Kyle
—Katie is sedated—
decides
whether or not
to resuscitate
their newborn child
a girl
a month later
at that child's funeral
while Margaret is teaching
because she is the only one
in the family who is working
her husband Harlan brings another woman
to the baby's funeral
brings her and they make googly eyes
brings her and smooches her

in front of all Margaret's friends
each-and-every one of them
call Margaret and this is how Margaret knows
she is getting divorced

3.

Aunt Mildred was a wealthy spendthrift spinster
before she died she arranged her funeral
to be as exact and proper and most importantly
as costly as her sister Vivian's was

Mildred made all the arrangements ahead of time
same headstone, same casket, same tidy concrete container
and, of course, the same funeral home, same viewing times
same prayer cards, same music so everything would be
  perfect

her youngest niece Karen however
spends her time at the viewing
not mourning, not crying
quietly in the restroom but

in her car drinking
a six or more of Busch her

husband having stocked the cooler
in the trunk for the long boring day ahead

Karen eventually passes out
on the sofa in the funeral parlor
several hours later she wakes up not
remembering where she is

or who is there—broadcasts
her husband's run-ins with family services—
Karen *was giving him* (her husband) *a blow job*
in the car while he was driving and

it got reported to the police that a child
was giving a blow job to an old man when
and this is the best part—
it turns out that I

was the one giving the blow job
not my daughter

Mildred's friends, Methodists,
former students—hands in their pockets,
eyes down, silent as they try and slip out the door
while the rest of the family tries to silence Karen

4.

It's 1981
you are going to your sister Chris' wedding
groomsmen in ivory tuxedos, bridesmaids
in floor length form-fitting red dresses
your niece is the flower girl, St. Gregory's church
the whole shebang and your sister
is wearing your wedding dress
now Chris has beautiful
Farrah Fawcett hair and
you do not but
you go and get a curly perm

the girl leaves the solution on too long
a patch of hair
from eye-to-eye to
the crown of your head
fries & breaks off
your mother tells you
not to worry—*your hair looks fine*
that *wigs aren't that costly*
and *they look pretty good*
you end up with a pre-punk
crew cut, sit in the last pew

hiding beneath a white straw fedora
& a pink tulle flower

GOING UNDER

A copperhead
colts down the path
his fragile fangs having
cooled in my grandmother's oniony
skin—did she hear
me drown:
as she lay neatly
on the grass her head
pillowed
on a fireman's red
handled ax?

In the deep
inner tube rounding
the 8 of the pool—sliding
through the black
my arms singing
to the cattails above;
did she hear my mother
bomb the surface drag

me back Wonder Bread wet
to the pale laughter
of my father?

JUNE BUG

for Bob Hise

I.

nocturnal scarab beetle
clumsy sheath-wing chafer
continues methodical march
down an auditory canal

II.

out out out she screams *out*
get the helicopter out of my ear OUT
the ER doctor thinks she's a psych patient

III.

She discovers she has cancer. Her vagina is renamed her primary
site. The next time tumors are found in her brain. Her secondary
site. Brain metastases. How is she supposed to endure all the terms
the teams of doctors throw at her?

Her Odds
        0.00131%.

IV.

she read somewhere the life of a beetle approaches 3 years
life she decides is about joys and struggles
a prayer chain, a phone tree is set up
individual meatloaves are baked

V.

no legs are lost
no hearing is lost
no forceps remove the prize

VI.

the likeness of a beetle
etched into a jewel, a talisman
of the soul

VII.

crickets dance
lightning bugs—fireflies—winged beetles
glow radiant in the twilight

LOSING MONDAY—

for HRP

when your husband's friend's number shows up
on your cell phone &

you are trying desperately
to flash through to the now missed call
when you redial before hearing the message

when they are both working the same conference
when you know it's bad news before you know for sure
when going to voice mail

when you go on-line to book a ticket to wherever the hell
he is this week
when his friend calls back and you connect

when the words spill to the ground
pooling like the blood from your husband's head
as he passed out—fell backwards onto
marble
splitting his skull
when 6 staples ka-chunk

ka-chunk ka-chunk ka-chunk
ka-chunk ka-chunk
ratchet into his cranium

when he loops the same stories when he
has no answers to the day or date or what happened
when his friends go to the ER and text you with updates

when a million years later your plane lands in Las Vegas
when after EEG, EKG, blood work
talk of syncope, retrograde amnesia, anterograde amnesia

when he didn't have a stroke heart attack seizure
when all he's lost is most of Monday
when nothing is conclusive

this is how you survive—

your friends, family, clients
when their calls, texts, emails declare

love & hope
commit to whatever you might need

TORNADO ALLEY

for Rita Jonas Lowell

whiplash after the moment
    of thunder before the storm
he says there was this noise a
zttttt

                  zttttt zttttt he says he
ran out the
door the *whoosh* the cursed
green sky jumbled the crack the burst of
the jolt of white—stink of ozone
the whole thing on fire he
ran out the door to just
to see what the noise was
whoosh whoosh to see
their single-wide ablaze he
ran back in her screams her
screams he tried to run back
in—she couldn't move—her
left side stroke-frozen he
tried to rip open the screen door
his hands angry-red ignited
the whole trailer engulfed in flames
like the papier-mâché piñata

their kids made in kindergarten he
says she
was there by the door—just inside
the screen—she was there screaming
screaming his name

DECOMPOSING DAD

Were you scared?
Groggy awakening after the knife—

plastic tentacles snaked down nose and throat—
wife? caressing the switch.

Vacation cut short—
with no place to shop   wife? clutching the will

did you flashback to your sister's death?
Sister plead no; wife? beseeching you to let 'er go.

Gasping for wife?
did you sincerely anticipate your life?

PRELUDE

Mom's new beau, Norm, hands her a Mason jar,
minimal Bloody Mary mix, max vodka, and a stalk of celery.
They were good to go.

Mom knocks the sludge off her boots
on the side of her daughter's hand-me-down Chevette.
Cardboard laid over the rusted-out floor.

She doesn't want to get it wet.
Cackling Norm crashes into the passenger door,
trying to crack the ice.

It won't start.
She pops the top.
Peers inside.

Battery's dead.
Bar's closed.
Walk or stay or call a cab.

They stand in the sleet and debate.
No hats, no gloves, forgetting to zip their jackets.
Mom's graying curls turn into Popsicles.

Norm rips open a pack of Camels,
his fingers cracked and yellowing.
Lights two, gives her one.

A week later mom is in the hospital,
pneumonia—small cell lung cancer—brain aneurism—
hospice.

POINTS OF ATTRACTION

in memory of Paul O. Williams

it didn't matter if
people thought I was his daughter
that I always said we're *just friends*

it didn't matter so long as
my feet were bound tight
in 4" leather high heels

as I stood and stood
my feet throbbing
to be released

at the end of the night if he would
walk me to my apartment
grasp my calf

slowly slip off
each stiletto
one at a time—

his hands
stroking
deep

thumbs submerged
into my soul

WRAITH

in memory of Dan Patterson

The great horned owl
messenger from some shadow land

pauses near my window
viewing his own reflection.

Did we date he used to joke
did I ever even ask you out?

No and yes.

He was a certain slant of light
a silver ribbon across emptiness

rain swirling into the night
all tunnels and vortex

he was the door into summer.

A DISTANCE TO BE TRAVELED

for Helen Hill, 1913 - 2002

The summer of '69
I was a plague of hormones—
a wrestler grappling her beer-belting dad.

Happenstance delivered me
to Helen's house on Rosemont Lane,
her flourishing cottage garden in La Jolla.

She promptly planted me like a fig
(a flower inverted into itself)
into a macrame of pancakes poured
from buckwheat batter,

rocks hounded from the ground
spun into jewels,
trips to the zoo, museums, galleries,
and Tijuana—

for *the* leather hat
my friends all loved,
my parents altogether loathed.

Snorkeling we caught fresh abalone.

I was cloistered in a thousand thousand
double paces—sunshine, sand,
golden-olive tan.

EN ROUTE

For weeks the prediction—snow
but always no snow
then at 3 AM when
I have a plane to catch—
snow! I run a shower,
change my flight and somehow
my boyfriend navigates the icy hills,
delivers me early to the airport. Alaska
puts me on my original 5:48 AM flight,
& after
a leisurely 6-hour SeaTac layover—
Wolfgang Puck egg white turkey
omelet, (2) large Beecher's drip coffees,
finish *The Walls Around Us,* & recharge
my phone I board, settle in to my 9C aisle seat when
a man with thinning ginger hair leans down, thrusts
his meaty hand at me, mumbles *Jeremy* tells me *just
shove on in, little lady, I'll take the aisle*
& after
I say no, after I explain I don't care
about his surgery, I explain he has no-idea
about my physical problems after he squishes

himself into the middle seat after he attempts
one-upping me even after I tell him *I am*
a writer, even after I say *funeral* even
after I say I have *never*
been to a monster truck show
he does not Shut Up, not until he consumes several
Dewar's, devours a box of Northwest
Picnic Snacks, salted almonds, a fig cookie not
even while I have my earphones in. Then and only
then he falls asleep party-hard—leaning
over-over-over onto me; my bony jabbing
elbow, my loud sighs, my shoving
his bulky shoulder, his looped 3 hour
nap between dazed wake-up and
back to sleep unapologetic *I-*
warned-you-you-should-
sit-in-the-middle stupor
and when we eventually land
I scamper off, offer no
direction, no goodbye, no
good luck, claim my
luggage, my middle of the road
hotel and prepare to deliver
the eulogy.

HOLDING UP

*Do not protect yourself from grief by a fence, but rather by your
friends.*

~Czech Proverb

for JR

Set yourself to a simple task.
Run hot soapy water in one side of a porcelain sink.
Pile in all the dishes, knives, forks, odd serving utensils.
Pile in lasagna dishes, crystal champagne flutes, tea cups.
Close your eyes.
A simple task.
Eyes closed, plunge your right hand into the mix—pull
something out, any one thing.
Set it into the other side of the sink.
Rinse with scalding water.
Do not place your hand in the disposal.
Do not mistake the switch for a light.
Be as careful as you can
avoid jagged edges
for surely something more has broken.
Salvage what you can.
Throw away what you cannot.
When you are out of hot water rinse away the blood

for surely something was rent again from the flesh.
Stack all that is cleansed neatly onto the drying rack.
Let your friends become towels.
Let them cushion the granite surfaces,
soak up the excess, buffer the friction—glass on glass.
A difficult task.
Open your eyes.
Let go.

I LOVE TEAMWORK, AS LONG AS I'M IN CHARGE

for N²

this magnet in the pile of presents I bought for you throughout
  the year
next year's birthday card—one so perfect I can hear you howl

remember the time the tornado siren went off so we pulled
into a Kmart, shopped for sundries—squabbled over the virtues
of some such product so loudly a woman behind us in the
  checkout line said

you girls remind me of me 'n my sister and
we burst into raucous laughter trying
to explain how we weren't actually sisters

remember how we fought over bathroom counter space in seedy
convention hotel rooms how we used to cram the room with
  people,
how after 10 years we settled on just the 2 of us

remember how we were going to live forever—outlive
our partners, move into a nursing home and chase young male
  nurses
how they'd surely kick us out for "unseemly" behavior

remember how you called knowing something was wrong, how
I called you knowing, how space and time did not matter and we
could always wait until then

remember how I was so focused on a friend's transition through
cancer, my promise to him to be there right before his death—
  to help
his wife, his children—to be there for them I remember

how I was so rooted with them that I did not hear you go

I remember how you spent your whole life searching for the light
  but you were already there

PERSIMMON

a cento for Susan Kenyon 1924-2018

She needed a prayer
to save the world
to praise

She remembered the old way
she found science inadequate
and philosophy

Becoming a woman
she is warned by Leto
she is torn

she dares
Exposure!
It is not entirely a new experience

not knowing what she knows
beyond her own skin
she links in and out

devastated at the thought of him in limbo
After her brother died she still hoped
to form him again

with its imitations in life
She rejected ghosts

in favor of life
and the not being
of death

She began to settle
for the long view
of family

for strange encounters
with others
with stones

illusions pleased her
Imperfections
informed her art

her colors
free her

Her children
coming to life
fill her nights

her days
with picnics
animate the chattels

She revisits wilderness
the forest
demons

leaves shelter
exposes herself
again

takes a talisman
walks the river
aware

she needs
not the old way
but a new view

to be free
for the old cause

gathering her material
she revisits death
Still whelmed

3

RIDING BACKWARDS ON TRAINS

after the killings, phosphorus
the orange of war, after
medals and stripes

back from *it* slamming
towards divorce, lost boys
their backs' to the future

hand on the clip
like my brother
the one we could never speak of

jailed in a time of war
my brother who had his own war
and lost

what the witness heard—

long pull of the whistle
tracks' metronome ratchet
bounded by sunrise

ELEGY FOR TWENTY-ONE MILLION WOMEN

he leaves no bruises no
shattered bones
only

fists of words
pounding over and over
echoing like the incubus;

luminous
she waits
for that concrete

thwack —
his assault
integral to her

leaving
this slow
internal

hemorrhage
of the soul

11×10^6

for Aunt Charlotte who gave me a paper clip necklace on
Thanksgiving Day

Eleven million paper clips collected
by an 8th grade class—
a clip for a life extinguished

by self-glorified xenophobia
and effective excessive force.
Lives memorialized

on the anniversary of Kristallnacht,
the night of broken glass,
the government sanctioned rape

and ravage of the Jews.
"Racially inferior" people sacrificed
depicted in the cumulation of genocided paper clips:

Jews	6,000,000.00
Gypsies, Gays, Disabled, etc.	5,000,000.00
Lives Lost in the Holocaust	11,000,000.00

in a railcar that wound its way
to concentration camps like Dachau to sort for selection:
forced labor and medical experimentation

infectious contagious diseases fevers, bone grafts, and neutering
the unlucky to extermination camps
at Chelmno, Belzec, Majdanek,

Sobibor, Treblinka,
or perhaps even Auschwitz-Birkenau
with its four (4) Zyklon B gas chambers.

By kids who had the courage to explore,
what does eleven million
look like?

MEANWHILE

after Wislawa Szymborska

One out of eight will. Someday.
Younger. Older.
It may develop.
It has developed.
It developed—but not in you.

You were not the one because you are still young.
Because no mother, no daughter, no sister developed it.
Because you never had it. Because your weight is normal.
Because you don't drink much. Because you had a child.
Because you had a child before you turned thirty.
Because you are male.

Fortunate you had your period after you were twelve.
Menopause before fifty-five, normal genes, a good diet,
a non-smoker, mindful meditation.
For those fortunate monthly self-examinations.

What would happen if you were the
twelve point five percent of the population,
the one out of eight?

Where does the math begin? Acquaintances,
second cousins twice removed, check-out clerks, drive thru
tellers, dental hygienists, that woman at the dog park?
Are they a part of your count?

A myriad of technicalities—
juxtapose your heart:
You? Me?

RECOUNTING THE DEAD

a found poem

after a vehicle packed with an improvised explosive device drove
    into the gate of his compound

after collapsing while on guard duty

after falling from a bridge, his vehicle was hit from behind by a
    civilian truck and left hanging off the side of the bridge

after two 122mm rockets were fired into his forward operating
    base

apparently fell into a canal and did not resurface

as a result of enemy action

as a result of hostile action

as a result of a non-combat injury

attempting to negotiate with armed men who were congregating
    on a road near a mosque after curfew

cause of death is under investigation

changing the tire on a Heavy Expanded Mobility Tactical Truck

    when the tire exploded

                drowned

due to hostile action

due to a non-hostile incident, the incident is under investigation

during a mortar attack when mortar rounds hit their camp

during a firefight with insurgents

fatal gunshot wounds while on guard duty at a propane distribution center

from an attack by small arms fire while conducting security of a weapons cache

from hostile fire

from injuries sustained from multiple gunshot wounds

from severe burns he received after his fuel-truck came under attack

from small arms fire after a dump truck on the side of the road was detonated while his military convoy passed by

inspecting soldiers on guard duty

inspecting a suspicious package when it exploded

last seen wading in the lake on the palace compound

lost at sea

manning a traffic control point when a vehicle came up to the checkpoint and two individuals got out requesting a medic for their sick friend, immediately following the request for help, they opened fire

non-hostile - illness - heat related

on patrol when the vehicle he was driving flipped over into a canal trapping him inside the vehicle

part of an ambulance crew transporting an injured soldier when the vehicle was hit by an RPG

participating in an air assault mission

participating in a small arms fire exercise on the range when a bullet ricocheted and ignited a fire in the building

participating in a raid at a suspected arms market when he was hit with shrapnel

patrolling a village when the vehicle was ambushed by RPGs

small arms fire wounds he received as his unit was engaging the enemy

struck by a stray bullet

thrown from his vehicle when the driver swerved to avoid an oncoming vehicle in another lane

vehicle ran into a ditch while trying to avoid a civilian vehicle

when a local resident threw a grenade over the wall

when a piece of unexploded ordnance accidentally detonated in the area he was working

when a tire on the 5-ton vehicle in which he was riding blew out and the vehicle overturned

when a suicide bomber detonated a car bomb next to his vehicle

when a vehicle-borne improvised explosive device detonated near his dismounted position during combat operations

when a vehicle pulled up and assailants fired on him

when an Avenger rolled over

when an explosion occurred near his convoy

when enemy forces ambushed their ground patrol

when he attempted to rescue the crewmembers

when he experienced severe chest pains

when he received sniper and rocket propelled grenade fire while securing a building

when he was shot by a suspected sniper

when he was struck by a forklift

when his camp came under mortar attack

when his M113 armored personnel carrier hit an antitank mine

when his patrol came under attack by rocket propelled grenades
and small arms fire

when his squad leader fell overboard he dived into the water and
did not surface

when his up-armored high-mobility-multi-purpose wheeled
vehicle was struck by rocket propelled grenades and small
arms fire

when his vehicle was attacked by small arms fire and an
improvised explosive device

when mortar rounds hit his living quarters

when their Bradley Fighting Vehicle came under attack by enemy
forces using small arms fire and rocket-propelled grenades

when his military vehicle was struck by a dump truck whose
driver had been shot while trying to run through a control
point

when his truck went off the road and rolled over because of
limited visibility and dangerous driving conditions

when he was electrocuted while performing routine generator
maintenance

when his military vehicle pulled off the road and apparently hit a
mine while on patrol

when the track of the tank he was in broke, the driver lost
control and the tank rolled off the bridge

while he was in a swimming pool when an electrical current
charged the water

THE PORCELAIN BOWL

Indifference is a weapon of mass destruction. ~Dennis Kucinich

Bloggers
like the witches of Macbeth
illuminate her wrath

envision the drowned—
black and bloated
martini olives bobbing

through the streets into once clean water;
those left—the living—with a brief pause
in their rape

wrap their dead in stolen
starched sheets, garbage bags, nothing;
march circuitous fetid streets.

Tens of thousands
praying for liberation.

A STRANGER ASKS FOR HELP WITH THE LETTUCE

in the boutique grocery co-op
he asks me if I know what his father is doing right now
in the city of St. Louis

    I say *oh I grew up there—he's BBQing*
no he says—*guess again & what high school did you go to*
    mmm—I couldn't guess—Ritenour

he removes his hand from my arm
—my father is golfing ha!
he backs away

of course—his father is not protesting
for Michael Brown, hasn't made a sign
Hands Up! Don't Shoot

is titillated about the unrest so far from home
how he can claim to be a liberal but we, he & I
we've been dancing around class the whole time

hell I hung out in Ferguson, got friends in Ferguson
got family in Ferguson but him—all he's got
is a daddy playing golf

/ & |

/ earthquake &
                aftershockaftershockaftershock & shock
residents sheltering in the street / & no
                                        food-water-medicine &
        & then & then the rains come &
    then & congruently

/ earthquake &
    avalanche [period]
                    tons & tons
        ice & air blast
                            & the mounting dead
    the mounting dead
    & dead & injured just
            | sound bites & trending |

THE FATE FOR WHICH WE MUST PREPARE

All warfare is based on deception. ~Sun Tzu

write your death poem

a huge fireball slams into Jupiter
hurricane season brings flooding, landslides, an enormous
    sinkhole
12 million cadmium-tainted Happy Meal glasses recalled

an impaled ocean endures
the corruption of oil
wetlands suffocate under thick coats of emollient

slick-soaked wildlife adorns the seaward limit of land
once white sand—sea turtles, brown pelicans, drown in tar tides
covered in unguent unable to eat or drink

if rescued, if they survive the eco disaster cleansing—
a complicated hour of scrubbing, rubbing, rinsing—
residual oil remains in their mouths, in their eyes

bite down on the mahogany red cherry
juice and pit—bite down to a curious cleft

the dull tremor, the slow actualization—the death of tooth and
  root

open your robe, take up your sword, make the plunge

CTRL-ALT-DEL

I unsent the message
undid the words
left them wholly
unfinished

I left them in limbo
unbalanced &
incomplete
unnerved

the shirt
unbuttoned
my bra unfastened
breasts undisturbed

as yet unconcluded
undestroyed—
prior to imaging I delete
the lump, mass, cavernous

unknowing

WHAT WE GIVE UP

we begin and end in the woods
old women and the trees

beyond the backyard
edging the cemetery
hide 'n seek

girl scouts making camp
stacking stones
finding our paths back

crossing the bitter cold of the river
removing leeches
at the trailhead

leaves of three
leaving them be
silence

girls blazing into bright red
poppies pistil stamen pollen
boys our marlins

we slip into heels
move indoors
form families

asleep in our boat
we acquiesce through time
the forest just out of sight

in the fall
out the front door
wherever we walk

riotous willows, oaks, elms
clone, root, take seed
sprout

pilot us back
to where we began

SALT

soaking in a tub braided with lemon verbena arnica
bath salts—a storm rolls in crashes
into the ocean, a gust ambers a seagull
freezes it in time

my toothbrush has broken, you
are asleep some other where
a pillar of the community an
old wound scabbing over

arnica in a cut causes scarring

twelve-year-olds purchase
White Lightning and Hurricane Charlie
bath salts laced
with mephedrone and
methylenedioxypyrovalerone
hallucinogens
just plain snorted, smoked, or
shot-up

get out their knives, slit their throats, bellies, random
body parts
in the end they
retrieve their parent's guns
barrels on tongues pull
the triggers

salt dries the cells until they are dead

I smacked my knee on the nightstand the
place between
soft puffy skin and the bone
leaving
an abrasion

SELF PORTRAIT AS OUR NATION'S CAPITOL

I am memorial and monument
I am bronze and marble, Martin Luther King
carved out of a mountain of white
the founding fathers my
wives and mothers—all women are add-ons they
are segregated, lonely and unvisited for it is my dogs
that are lovingly bronzed beside me
I am 37 individual police units
I am chain link fence, short, tall

permanent, movable
I am surrounded by concertina wire
I am Jersey barriers and
concrete
you can eat off my streets—
my un-homed disappeared
the West is on fire
much of the country parched though
my lawns are dug up, spruced up
fitted for sprinklers
I am perfectly manicured
I am rules and signs I tell you
do not enter—restricted—cross

do not cross, park, pay by
phone; my signs tell you where to pick up your car
when it is towed; signs simultaneously blink
red 10-9-8... command wait-wait-wait
I am surveillance
video cameras adorn me inside and out
so numerous they have become nearly invisible
I am Metro stations poorly lit, poorly ventilated
trains every 6 or 15 or 24 minutes depending
during rush hour commuters, visitors crush into me
to my veterans visiting their ghosts
people push—throng—clash cacophony
until I am gorged
I am guns carried concealed
no one looks me in the eye
I am Liberty
Justice
Freedom
Equality

I am monument
I am memorial

4

THE MOON IS A HARSH MISTRESS

Is a virus self-aware? Nyet. How about oyster? I doubt it. A cat?
Almost certainly.
~Robert Heinlein

She is a full milk carton with no new listings
children gone missing—her beloved
felines having faded into a chill
predawn on tiny fog feet.

The moon doesn't scour the streets trilling her child's name
flood the streets with flyers
call the neighbors
offer a reward for a return.

No.

She waxes laconic remits muted light
sparkling into shadows beams sent
under upturned lawn furniture radiates
through the thick thick ivy

broods. Where is her little lost one?

FOR A MOMENT

Ants. 60 bazillion strong. Crawling in the sill tricksy, around the kitty condo back to the wall and then onwards to the cats' bowl of kibble. Though I am a peaceable person I draw the line. Rain a chemical crusade on their droning masses. On their seeming forever war. Sugary traps filled and refilled.

I look out the window at my 3 black cats gathered around a small black bird its chest heaving up-and-down up-and-down. Go out to rescue the bird that has been flipped—a winged pancake. See the tiny bird anatomy. Intestines like the worms my father and I used to fish with at Forest Park. It still breathes.

I should kill the dead bird. I want to kill the dead bird. Too late, I would have killed the dead bird.

I go inside to change out another ant trap, glare out the window at the cats. They crowd a small grey mouse. It is not a vole. It is dead. One cat nudges it with his left paw. One cat looks up at me, licks the mouse from tail to snout. Never breaks eye contact.

I should gather the bits and bury them, make a shrine, place stones and candles. In the silence, hold a vigil.

> whispering
> between life and death
> one bud then another

RAVEN SONG CROW SONG

in memory of La Femme Nikita 1993-2011

Last week a raven in a fir tree serenaded me with a lilting
song;
I didn't know they sang.

Yowling. Eyes, starbursts of pain.
Nikita always knows when I am sick or injured
lies on whatever hurts. My cat is dying.

She sits with me, a paw on my thigh.
We stare out the window at the parade of crows—
seven who have come to gather up seed, millet, peanuts.

I wish she could have heard the raven's lullaby.
It would have made her young again.

a stone
near the koi pond
for Django

TOPAZ, THE GRUMPINATOR

He quit eating.
He quit drinking.
He dreamed me his death.
So I'd know it was time.

Emaciated.
Wobbly and bent.
Falling off things. Or just simply falling.
Yowling non-stop that last year.

Orange and white,
a talkative guy, who
used to be spry.

I took his picture,
a lock of his fur,
made a print of his paw.

Then, hardest of all,
I made the call.

One shot to calm him.
I wrapped him in a towel,
held him on my lap.

Gentle rain of oak and maple leaves,
acorns plunking at my feet,
and in the fleeting sunlight—

one shot to still his heart.

POLICE—DO NOT CROSS

because leaving early
because intermittent mixes snow rain
because the crush of after
holiday traffic
because bumper-to-bumper
thump-crunch ahead
because lights but no sirens & then
because a long-ass freight train
because all the cut-throughs are
because I heard it on NPR—
a bird sanctuary hostaged
because 3 firs need felling
because PT, because the old one no longer condescends
to eat—even Beech-Nut chicken, beef or turkey baby food &
therefore an overdue unscheduled end-of-life
conversation with the vet
because now I was
I am late

IN VIEW OF THE FACT THAT; CONSIDERING; INASMUCH AS

perhaps she should have known
perhaps she did know
did not know precisely

perhaps she could have pieced
the clues, his constant treadmilling
cleaning up the house

putting his life in order
she would have guessed
did think it from his probable

cancer the tumors &
she was glad they were benign though
nightly she dreamt he died

did not tell him
not wanting to give voice
to Death

leaving her
the Steller's Jay the cat brought in almost
but not quite alive

AFTER THE RAPTURE

a found poem

This is what will happen for all pets registered with us immediately after the Rapture—

1. Our non-Christian administrators will activate our rescue plan.

2. Volunteers will be alerted immediately by email and telephone that they have been activated.

3. Pets will be assigned to our Volunteer Pet Caretakers based upon location and other factors.

4. Our administrators and Volunteer Pet Caretakers will do whatever it takes to find and rescue your pets. If they are unable to reach a Volunteer Caretaker in your area for whatever reason, our administrators will communicate with local animal organizations, like the Humane Society, to

advocate for your pet's rescue and
care.

INSATIABLE

Raven cat,
starving, world revolving around
him cat—leader of the Army of Darkness
biting growling throwing-up cat
going to the vet cat
cat who we were positively not
keeping cat
that tricked us into rescuing him
cat who was going to be named Loki but couldn't because
my brother-in-law already had a cat named that and
we didn't worry too much about the naming but
sitting at the Westmoreland Animal Hospital
the vet escalating from your cat doesn't look too sick
to 3 hours in a linoleum tiled room with one chair
and one more test and then more precisely
"having to do research" on the problem
leading to IV fluids, antibiotics, an overnight stay
$1,002.56 for colitis because of something he ate (bird)
and now it's a teaspoon of prescription wet
more bland and boring than baby food
every
two hours

for a week

or

as

long

as

it

takes.

LIGHT LIKE A STAR

for Jeff Williams

1.

Remember that morning? Anticipation
before the ashes—how Elvis wants
to be let out—how I want to flee

the battleship sky carnivorous we
zig-zag down tender dry
hills before

eucalyptus explode and Oakland
is scarlet.

2.

a torrid Midwest sun forces us into the pool
diving for pennies in the deep end turquoise
the last time we were invited over
the last time before you melted
to nothing and your daughter
called the ambulance
to cart you away

3.

As the storm fractures acorns
Elvis jumps into a complex pool.
He is the only thing you have
left.

FLAME POINT

n memory of Tessa

carrier—car—locked door
she always hated containment
my last California cat
buried beneath firs

NO MORE SKY DIVING

one minute he is atop the dryer
trying to jump catawampus
into the exploding laundry chute
the next there is only silence & you have not
screeched out *God Damn It Dorian*
Don't (fill in the blank) once this afternoon
which is odd
so you go in search of the little guy
who is peacefully sleeping on his heated bed
mid-day—in reasonable weather
which is very odd
& since he must be faking lethargy
you break out the beloved salmon snacks
catnip, a can of cat food, a can of real
tuna & picking him up nets you a growl
& a nip which is how you know you *are* going
to the vet tomorrow & that you are no longer
going out for New Year's Eve celebrations
& you are glad you didn't buy those new shoes—
STAT work-ups, fluids, pain medication(s)
tech time, vet time buys you a 105° fever-fighting-off-infection
        diagnosis

he's home & two days later he's still
not eating & oh so bitey & you're off
to the ER with your sharp crabby kitty
who turns out to have broken his sternum
& you give him all the salmon snacks & spendy stinky
mackerel & sardines he can consume
as you conjure a stalking the crow-on-the-roof-top jump—chase
the brazen squirrel to the crown-of-the-black-oak fall—
vicious buck, pregnant doe hoof—hell hound paw—
Manimal steel-toed boot—the resounding
concussion—the splinter
of the long flat bone that joins ribs to cartilage
to safeguard his teenage heart

WHEN THE TRINE BETWEEN THE MOON AND MERCURY TEMPERS THE VIBE

sometimes the phone is a duende moon
an oppressive humidity pooling on lilac leaves

squalls complex incantations
to ward off extinction

I offer Kool-Aid colored sunflowers
starlight etched on yesterday's sun-drenched chair

in the car over Bluetooth I hear how Abigail Poundcake
is listless and dying and my friend does not know what to do

in this disaster she's driven to a vet who isn't there and no one
but me answers the call

I stop the car then—the thrum
of dark-eyed juncos in dogwood blossoms

OCTOBER RAINS

I become the tide
            ebb and flow [opening]
      cats come in [and closing]
         cats go out [each
         doorway] into rain
                they will not
go around to the back door
            cracked open a smidge &
         it has warmed enough
                    for that but they are insisting
on summer or sunshine
                    or drought
      I cannot find the dead bird
            only feathers
                    white down on the landing
      two flight feathers on the kitchen floor
and a flurry of black down—
      underneath the dining room table
                    there was no alarm

no clatter of bells no
      change in the background noise
            of morning no smash no chitter
   only this spatter of nuthatch feathers
         perhaps it has escaped with yesterday's mouse
        into a vent

5

GHOST RANCH

walk the labyrinth

between flagstone / river rock

prickly pear / fluxweed's pale petals

mediations / compass points

heartfelt truths with stones

blue lace agate settles

in the cup of coffee

gusty winds may exist

IN MY SKY OF SAND

I'll make you as terrible as you desire: windblown
moonbeam, amethyst,
cockroach, a pallbearer reaches for a necklace.
Widowhood has her season—floats
laid out like a painting. Unspoken
as long as it is now. Regret

their toothy grins, all malice. Regret
what others will find by indecision windblown,
on streaky slates unspoken,
a transmigration of souls neither tourmaline nor amethyst.
Emptiness filled by pebbles floats
each of us, shamed by a necklace.

This slaughter—a killing frost necklaced
around your throat snip-snip. Regret
swallows itself in a perpendicular spark, floats
your head against a lavish beacon windblown.
The sharpened edge of guilt, the fracture of amethyst
every moment so intense water cannot relate unspoken;
everything some danger unspoken.

Skirt along the hem of a necklace
flaws—bring out your beauty, my Amethyst.
Destitute of motivation regret
the soul that refuses to disclose its windblown
location. This wet night's journey floats
not anticipating any leave-taking. Floats?

Which is it, I wonder unspoken.
I would open up my wrists windblown
to be something some nuance some subterfuge to
 the necklace
that bore my regret.
Obsession is a chaste amethyst

whose shriek surges seductive, Amethyst,
a drunkard who loves serene decay and floats
kissed clean—free of regret
with nothing to kindle you unspoken.
Your name whispered in the spokes of a necklace
forlorn, apology never more than windblown.

Tempest, locust, amethyst you are a plague new and unspoken—
a conjure that floats too full of words to string a necklace.
Regret is a cobweb on fire, all that I do not want—windblown.

IDA BY MOONLIGHT

after a painting by Bill Rane

a faint image—a near-living design
expanding and contracting
she flows into every viable organism

lost and reappearing
interwoven
a ghost fugue

a Sylph—ephemeral vapor
upon the breath
all thought

without the weight
of the world
she guards

the gates
to the mortal plane

ELEGY ON THE DEATH OF A FRIEND

for Patricia K. (Grainge) Phillips 1957-2018

after an eclipse
—the blue moon supersized
having no more business in this world

she died

friendship forged in girlish dreams
boys, bibles, education
and escape

between us lies
deafening white space
untold stories, erasing ink

examine what lies beneath

Mom, Lowell, Max—
Debbie, Doug, Alan,
Charlie and Beth

road trips, revivals, hoofing 2 miles
there and back and there
Pineview to E. Milton

she wrote in my yearbook—
to a stupid dunce // my coolest friend //
sort of

we caught fire: jeans, tin foil
cook stoves, we had vicious fights
over stupid boys: sin

she won our last stupid fight
taking the moral high ground
saved my life by speaking out

through the drift of space
and time, daughters Melissa and Emily
the grands Alex and Macy, love, laughter

weaving the heavy scent of illness
and other demons, redemption
a slow mending and now

ashes to ashes
she catches the wind
rises, towards the light

AFTER THE EULOGY

When all has been said, when we blow our noses, retire to the kitchen, remove plastic wrap, shove the proper serving utensils into steaming pans of mostaccioli and lasagna, cold cuts, cheese slices, potato salad, salad-salad, baked beans, fruit and veggie trays, ranch dressing, Rice Krispies treats, chocolate Scotcheroos, cheesecakes, homemade cookies, when we've had our fill and are milling about or sitting down. Before we leave the church. When we are breathing again and functional. When a random guy in a black leather jacket puts his arm around me, tells me I am *still hot*, recalls my burnt orange Toronado, tells me the years have been kind, when he asks me if I'm happy. When I say *yes*. When he asks *isn't that your sister*. When I say *yes* and *she's married*. When he thinks about it and says *...well don't you have another*. When I say *yes* and *she is single ...* and *she would surely love some company—though she does have dementia but she does recall the past vividly.* When I still can't conjure him / our past. A week later when I feel bad that perhaps I should have heard his story, when I contact a friend, she tells me how he shot his father a couple of years ago (*non-fatal injuries*) and he's *just hangin' around* but when pressed she recollects that *at least he didn't go to jail.*

CATCHING UP

FaceTiming with my sister at her memory care facility, Day 120

she asks—*how's Leon*   dead
—*how's your sick friend, Marie*   dead
Baby (her cat)   dead   & then *Socks*   dead
    Dorian (my cat)   dead   *well then—*
what about Mike, he's you know   fine,
double bypass & stents but he'll live
    Pat, Grandpa Bill   dead   *Belvedere wait*
he's from a long time ago so he's dead, right   yes
& yes & mom & dad too & now she's about
to cry & I laugh and say sister it's great you
are remembering the dead—someday someone
will remember us &   she laughs out loud
    sister then will you buy me a new bra

A GRIM REAPER

At the border between the worlds
he could be sighted. Some confused him
with Lucifer, some with that other guy. But
he was just the messenger—doing his 9-5.

He was a lion, a scorpion, a snake, he was
invisible, he wore a veil, a sword, a sickle
and an hourglass, a scythe, he was a drummer,
a dancer, a beautiful girl, he was ashes.

He wished he could ditch his metaphor
maybe swap the scythe for a Glock and an iPhone,
or some other smart phone, for the hourglass
'cause man that thing is huge. Just once

he'd like to go about his day in a snug
pair of jeans and a ball cap.

"COUSIN" LARRY

flew in from Jersey
hadn't been back to LA
for 47 years Larry was

sporting his notorious hot pink &
turquoise madras-print short-sleeve shirt
& navy-blue pleated trousers

at his nephew's Celebration of Life
at The Beverly in Hollywood, in the garden
Larry crisscrosses the grass, plants—uncousinly kisses

on all the women—says *hey you sure are*
good lookin', at 2 in the afternoon blares
there's a full open bar—the 5th wife's back home ...

afterwards at the family dinner
he TALKSOVER questions posed by
the hard-of-hearing 85-year-

old mother who has a burning question
about Caller-IDs Larry bombards us *don't
bother answering, the old ones never*

*remember anything anyhow go ahead, let them live
at home, alone, they're gonna die (((soon))) anyways
for fucksake it's not like they listen*

WHAT THE DEAD SEE

after a photo by Emily Wilensky

bedrooms full of ghosts
prepared for a storm
glancing off sharp edges

outcasts suicides remnants lovers
answerable to many sorrows
the dead want

to be provoked
they want
atonement

day by day the living segue
away—until the long fallen are
utterly forgotten

and yet, there you are
on the half-plane of convergence

THE BIRD OF TIME

*Thou remembered haply, thou rememberest when I said to
thee that holy word, 'Opportunity is the fairest, opportunity
the lightest-footed of things; opportunity may not be
overtaken by the swiftest bird in air.' Now lo! all thy flowers
are shed on the ground.* ~Thymocles

In the chill space
where the dead
and the living endure

a cuckoo beckons you
with melancholy.
He sings and sings and sings

a cabernet warble.
His voice an echo
of your torture—lobbed

across the ethereal
until you thirst for the dirt,
to be wrapped in raw umber.

143

NOVEMBER

the rain settles in
a constant   giving way
to bluster, downpour
stop & go thunder
not yet quite an onslaught
I drive up the 5 in the
company of   ghosts—
overwintering fields amber
copper-vermillion swirls
   bittersweet halos, massing bleak
clouds   ghosts   rusted
hawks atop fence posts
a lone blue heron pirouettes
in peridot sedge
the radio, NPR drones on &   & on   ghosts
recalibrating GPS   ghosts

I deliver books, meet my friend's mom
   ghosts   I'm mauled by border collie
kisses   ghosts   Sherman Alexie's
   ghosts are following me
the chronic embrace a

collective   ghosts'   brimmed
stories unfold in slow time
a nod to my mother, a recalling
recanting, recollection   yesterday was
her birthday, my hoop of   ghosts
multiplies & splits
an earnest cancer   this
day I have no
need   no want for more
company

ON THE EDGE OF DUSK

in memory of Karen Locke 1945-2018

I think you would love it here in winter—
15 miles of white knuckles over the pass
the drive through the snow
not quite bad enough for chains

I think you would love the stillness
of Summer Lake in January
the sudden onslaught of winds
whipshattering through the high desert

tossing a solitary leaf ramshackle
across the field—you didn't plan
to fall a second time to spend
your last days bound to machines

last night on the edge of the marsh
I saw you amble through the tall grass
waive an old-timey lantern above your head
—*farewell*

a great horned owl perches on
the willow by my cabin, sings

to her fledgling in a call and response
whoo-whoo-whoo—hoot-hoot hoot-hoot

at daybreak a fog rolls in
and coyotes break into a mournful dirge

APPROXIMATION

      walking the road

     connecting confessions

ungiving moments

              her thoughts

   pebbles&sand

     concretions she

just   starts   screaming   gravels

    against being

      time unlit

PROPORTIONAL RELATIONSHIPS

Death A sells "small" glitches after surgery, car crashes, wrong-place wrong-time bullets, massive heart attacks for unforeseen abrupt cessation of all life functions. Death A accommodates spending every breath with intention, spontaneity, fractured last words, irreversible choices, shocked friends searching for what-ifs. A barn owl hoots outside the bedroom window.

Death B sells seemingly unfatal falls, end-stage cancer, bit-by-bit strokes, dementia, long lingering departures. Death B includes, perhaps, closure, becoming a ghost before you are a ghost, hospice, Do Not Resuscitate, final farewell, a white-tailed kite soaring over the delta.

Death A and Death B introduce circumstance versus free will, the multitude of unstoppable possibilities, a phone ringing late in the night, logistical problem solving, loved ones making unplanned-for decisions, division of property, burial or cremation, last wishes, last words, a new dress.

Which Death offers the better deal?

UNTITLED

for MJ

shotgun—suicide

BANG!

the writer's son commits
to the trigger, marries the lead
through the back of his skull
not
not

not not not

no not unexpected
not anything the writer will be able
ever be able to withstand he
(the writer)
ripens into multiple despair
surly fonts ; finds smoldering
incorrigible grammar an
evolution
amalgam of run-on-sentences

bangBangBANGS his oblivion—he-him they is/are
as unreliable
narrator

CUMULONIMBUS

for MDK

along a path pale flowers shimmer in a ghost tree
fledglings make a crown
a chorus of crows

lulls you
into the calm

from the wetlands a snowy owl lifts its wings to take flight
your father falls, a simple thing—
a fall, a feather, hospice

the lull, the ache
that jolt of lightning

NOTES

"Persimmon," is a Cento, all lines in this poem are all titles from Susan Kenyon's book, *Petal on the Tongue.*

"Recounting the Dead," from antiwar.com 10/24/11.

"Self Portrait as our Nation's Capitol."

1. When I was married my then in-laws lived in DC so for 20 years I took DC for granted, I'd pop in, catch up with the family, eat home-baked cinnamon rugelach or (on the holidays) apricot hamantaschen, go to an art opening, or to the Mall to check out the newest museum.

2. My then father-in-law, Mort, was a DC lawyer, he wrote part of the GATT (General Agreement on Tariffs and Trade).

3. When I got divorced I still stayed very much in touch with my in-laws, with my ex's whole family because they (unlike my own family) were the awesome family who supported the arts, had college degrees and loved to discuss politics.

4. When my father-in-law died I flew to DC to his celebration of life.

a. I took my new beau. He is a Marine, a Vietnam veteran, a poet. He'd never been to DC. I called my Congressman, Peter DeFazio, and arranged a Parks Tour to see all the national monuments (I would very much recommend this if you ever go to DC). We also went to the Smithsonian—rather 2 or 3 of them. We rode the Metro, went to Arlington Cemetery, we went to the Pentagon. We did not go on a White House tour because the Pope was in town.

5. So how did I come to write this poem? It took a while, its impetus is complicated. It was written for Mort who had a wicked sense of humor, who loved and valued honesty and who took the time and showed me his neighborhood; and for my new partner, Roy, who served his country with loyalty but was treated horribly when he returned—a man who could barely speak at seeing the Memorial and for me because I saw DC with a whole new set of eyes. This poem was written because of the 45th President who was occupying the White House. This poem was written to get you to vote in every election.

"After the Rapture," from
http://www.aftertherapturepetcare.com/ .

ACKNOWLEDGMENTS

Grateful acknowledgment is made to the editors of the following journals and presses for first publishing these poems or earlier versions of them:

The Alabama Writer's Conclave, "No More Skydiving,"
    http://www.alabamawritersconclave.org/winners.html

Anti-Heroin Chic, "Ghost Ranch," http://heroinchic.weebly.com

Cascadia Review, "A Stranger Asks for Help with the Lettuce,"
    http://cascadiareview.org/

The Cherry Blossom Review, "Wraith,"
    http://www.geocities.com/thecherryblossomreview Fall '07

Cirque, "The Fate for Which We Must Prepare"

Clearfield Review, "The Bird of Time"
    http://www.freewebs.com/clearfieldreview

Dogplotz, "An Invisible Fluvial Zoo,"
    http://www.dogzplot.com/submit.html

Elohi Gadugi Journal, "Riding Backwards on Trains,"
http://egjournal.org/

Everyday Poems, "Heritability,"
http://www.everywritersresource.com/poemeveryday/

Every Day Other Things, "What the Dead See,"
http://everydayotherthings.com

The Feline Muse, "Topaz, The Grumpinator,"
http://www.thefelinemuse.com

The FemLit Magazine, "Some Assembly May be Required,"
https://thefemlitmagazine.wordpress.com

Filling Station, "In My Sky of Sand," Canada Issue 49 2010

Flywheel Magazine, "Raven Song Crow Song,"
http://www.flywheelmag.com

Gargoyle Magazine #73-74, "Proportional Relationships" and
"When the Trine Between the Moon and Mercury Tempers
the Vibe"

Gold Man Review, "Olly Olly Oxen Free"

HeArts Desire, HeArt's Desire a Poetic Complement to the Adobe Art Gallery Exhibition, "A Distance to be Traveled," elizapress, Hayward, CA 2007

The Incongruous Quarterly, "Insatiable," http://incongruousquarterly.com

The Inflectionist Review, "Approximation," http://inflectionism.com

Lady Ink, "June Bug," http://www.ladyinkmagazine.com

L'Allure des Mots, "Points of Attraction," http://lalluredesmots.com

Mad Poet's Society, "Meanwhile," 07/01/06 Volume 20, PA Finalist "Meanwhile," MoonPathPress, *Willingly Would I Burn*, 2012

Oregon Writer's Colony, *Anthology: In Our Own Voices*, "The Porcelain Bowl," 08/06/06

2019 Playa Anthology "On the Edge of Dusk"

Poe Little Thing, "Going Under," http://blackriverpublishing.homestead.com/Poelittlething.html

Perigee, A Grim Reaper," http://www.perigee-art.com/ Volume IV Issue IV, Internet (May/June/July 2007)

Poeming Pidgeon, *In the News,* "Self Portrait as Our Nation's Capitol," 04/01/18 and as part of the art/audio installation Pictures of Poets http://picturesofpoets.com/Poets/laura-lehew/

poeticdiversity, "The Moon is a Harsh Mistress," http://www.poeticdiversity.org Internet (August 2008).

Poetry Landfill, "Possessing No Physiological Function," http://poetrylandfill.com/?page_id=77,

Poetry Now, "11 x 10^6" and "Elegy for Twenty-One Million Women" Sacramento

The Quotable, "Recounting the Dead," http://thequotablelit.com and "Recounting the Dead," at 24 Sandy Gallery, installation: *Welcome to My World - artists take on the world* 11/14/2011

The Rattlesnake Review—Medusa's Kitchen, "A Face Held in Darkness," June 2010

The Rattlesnake Review, "Prelude," rattlesnakepress.com

Seven Circle Press, "3 Days Prior to April Fools Through Friday the 13th—A Fortnight of Reckoning in the Year of the Dragon," Seven Circle Press-1st place; nominated for a pushcart 2014

The Starving Artist, "The Sad Man," http://www.the-starving-artist.com

Thresholds, "Ida by Moonlight," Eugene, OR

The Tiger's Eye Poetry Journal, "Imagine,"

The Tiger's Eye Journal, Three Funerals and a Wedding, 05/16/13

The Tonopah Review, "Light Like a Star," http://www.tonopahreview.com

The Tule Review, "October Rains," Sacramento 06/05/13

Wild Age Press, "Salt," 06/15/12 The Anything Goes Contest: 2nd Place

Willawah Journal, "After the Eulogy" and "In View of the Fact That, Considering; Inasmuch as," http://willawawjournal.com Winter 2018

And with gratitude to poetry friends, mentors, and places that have sustained and inspired me over the years while this book took shape:

To the members of the 1st and 3rd Thursday group who provided me with valuable critiques and support over the many years: Quinton Hallett, Karen Locke, Nancy Carol Moody, Sharon Lask Munson, Keli Osborn, Jenny Root, Colette Tennant, Ingrid Wendt, and Harriot West;

To the supporters of and administrators at Hypatia-in-the-Woods, Playa, the Montana Artists Refuge, and Soapstone, for time and space to read and write and revise in places of serenity;

To Dean Davis for his splendid author photograph;

To the editors **Samuel Nichols, Esme Howler, S.R. Stewart** and the rest of Unsolicited Press for their enthusiastic acceptance of this manuscript and hours devoted to making it shine;

To Quinton Hallett and Nancy Carol Moody for gracious and unerring eyes ferreting out errors and polishing lines;

And always to Roy.

CPSIA information can be obtained
at www.ICGtesting.com
Printed in the USA
LVHW091924110222
710698LV00004B/204

9 781956 692068